Also by Hart Seely

Pieces of Intelligence:
The Existential Poetry of Donald H. Rumsfeld

2007-Eleven:
And Other American Comedies
(with Frank Cammuso)

O Holy Cow! The Selected Verse of Phil Rizzuto
(with Tom Peyer)

Mrs. Goose Goes to Washington

NURSERY RHYMES FOR THE POLITICAL BARNYARD

Hart Seely

Free Press

New York   London   Toronto   Sydney

FREE PRESS
A Division of Simon & Schuster, Inc.
1230 Avenue of the Americas
New York, NY 10020

First Free Press hardcover edition June 2007

FREE PRESS and colophon are trademarks of Simon & Schuster, Inc.

For information about special discounts for bulk purchases,
please contact Simon & Schuster Special Sales:
1-800-456-6798 or business@simonandschuster.com

DESIGNED BY ERICH HOBBING

Manufactured in the United States of America

1   3   5   7   9   10   8   6   4   2

Library of Congress Cataloging-in-Publication Data
Seely, Hart.
Mrs. Goose goes to Washington: nursery rhymes for
the political barnyard/Hart Seely.
p. cm.
1. Mother Goose—Parodies, imitations, etc. 2. Political poetry, American.
3. Humorous poetry, American. 4. Verse satire, American. I. Title.
PS3619.E355M77 2007
811'.6—dc22   2007000549
ISBN-13 978-1-4391-6721-2
ISBN-10 1-4391-6721-4

To Janice,
for putting up with me.

CONTENTS

1.

"I know an old party that swallowed a war
Don't know what for, it swallowed a war"

The White House

Mother Bush Had a House

Mother Bush had a house,
'Twas built in the glades,
Where she worked all day,
Employing her maids.

She had a son, George,
A fine-looking male,
He was not very bright,
But still made it to Yale.

He launched a career,
To the White House he got;
"See, Mother," said he,
"I have not been for naught."

But George knew one matter,
That bothered his mom,
Folks still blamed his father
For botching Saddam.

He vowed that his father
Would yet be revered,
And he crafted a plan
So his dad would be cleared.

3

And George kept his vow,
As his mom knew he would.
He screwed up so badly,
His father looked good.

Rub-a-Dub-Dub

Rub-a-dub-dub,
Three men in the tub.
The Cheney, the Rummy, the Commander-in-Dummy,
They all believed they had the will.
They never thought we'd be there, still.

Rub-a-dub-dub,
Three men in the tub.
The Leaker, the Mistaker, the Quagmire-Maker,
They all believed they'd done the math.
They never thought they'd take the bath.

Hear This, You Evil Tyrants

Hear this, all evil tyrants,
As you plot foul attacks:
Condoleezza Rice has pledged
To stop you in your tracks.

She won't use UN sanctions,
She's moved beyond that phase.
Her office uses harsher means
To make you change your ways.

For starters, if she learns about
Your plans to build a bomb,
She'll send out to your neighbors
Doctored photos of your mom.

On walls of public restrooms
She'll tape your business card.
She'll fill a bag with dog doo,
And then light it in your yard.

She'll call you on your cell phone,
While at a soccer game,
She'll page "Anita Mantokiss"
And have you shout the name.

She'll hand you trick binoculars
That blacken both your eyes.
She'll call up nearby pizza joints,
And send you fifty pies.

She'll shorten up your bed sheet,
And hide your TV clicker,
She'll slip Viagra in your soup,
And water in your liquor.

She'll coat your phone with Super Glue,
And call you every hour.
She'll flush the toilet several times
While you are in the shower.

She'll lead you to a bleacher seat
Where all the paint is wet.
She'll send you a subscription
To the *Man/Boy Love Gazette*.

So dictators, take notice,
From China to Brazil:
Do not test the U.S.A.!
Just look at Kim Jung Il.

George Tenet

George Tenet, on advice,
Rushed one night to Doctor Rice,
Somewhere near the Senate,
Poor George Tenet.

George Tenet, businesslike,
Said Bin Laden planned a strike,
So did he present it.
Poor George Tenet.

George Tenet walked away,
Nothing did she hear him say,
All he did was vent it.
Poor George Tenet.

George Tenet, now outside,
Has a medal, yet no pride.
He did not prevent it.
Poor George Tenet.

Itsy-Bitsy Scooter

Itsy-bitsy Scooter
Climbed up the oval spout,
Down came the leaks
That brought the agent out.
Out came the probe
That tried to find the blame,
And the itsy-bitsy Scooter
Climbed up the spout again.

Itsy-bitsy Scooter,
Went up into the Mall,
Down came the word,
That he would take the fall.
Out came the trial
That played across the land,
And the itsy-bitsy Scooter,
Declined to take the stand.

Itsy-bitsy Scooter
Went up the legal route,
Down came the verdict:
Guilt, beyond a doubt.
Down went the aide
To suffer in the end;
And the itchy-twitchy Cheney,
Had shot another friend.

The King Is Delighted

The king is delighted.
Rove's not indicted!
Go tell the queen.
They found Karl clean!

The king is elated,
Our beloved Rove skated!
Go tell the Speaker.
Karl's not the leaker!

The king is in clover.
Rove's ordeal is over!
Party tomorrow.
It's a great day for Karl!

The king's in a flurry.
Rove won't face a jury!
Break out the ale.
Karl's not going to jail!

Feel the excitement.
No Rove indictment!
Everyone, sing.
Karl's still our king!

Tony Snow, How Does It Grow?

Hey, ho! Tony Snow!
How long does your bony nose grow?

An inch for tax rates on upper classes,
An inch when you discuss greenhouse gasses.

An inch for torture as terror prevention,
An inch when you scrap the Geneva Convention.

An inch for budgets and jobless data,
A foot when you link Iraq to al-Qaeda.

An inch for Clinton, Kerry, and Gore,
A mile when you claim we're winning the war.

It grows every question and every rebuttal.
When you look up, you can sniff the space shuttle.

This Young Man

This young man, he played one.
He played knick knack from Vietnam,
With a Guard-track, dodge-the-draft,
Leave the boy alone.
This young man stayed safe at home.

This young man, he played two.
College classes sliding through,
With the Skull-and-Bones, frat-clones,
Pour the boy a brew.
This young man went driving stewed.

This young man, he played three.
High in Harken Energy,
With a quick-drop, ditch-the-stock,
Dodge the SEC.
This young man got off scot-free.

This young man, he played four.
Major league investment score.
With a big-wheel, insider-deal,
Give the boy his dream:
Owner of a baseball team.

This young man, he played five.
Led the "Build a Ballpark!" drive.
With a kickback, special-tax,
Line up is the best,
Also-rans in A.L. West.

This young man, he played six
Sold the team to Thomas Hicks.
With Clear Channel, money-funnels,
Texas needs his flare,
He's "Governor Electric Chair."

This young man, he played seven.
Has a backer up in heaven.
With the right-wing, Christian thing,
He's the favored Son.
This young man took Washington.

This young man, he played eight.
Sent the Army to Kuwait,
With a yellow-cake, total fake,
We'll win it in a walk.
This young man attacked Iraq.

This young man, he played nine.
New Orleans would be just fine.
With a Cat-4, at-the-door,
Counting up the dead.
Frowned when he flew overhead.

13

This young man, he played ten.
In Iraq and Afghanistan,
With a knick, knack, paddy whack,
A double Vietnam.
This young man's come rolling home.

2.

"This little lobby went to Hastert
This little lobby went to Blunt"

Congress

Republicans and Democrats

What are little Republicans made of?
Bushes and Quayles,
And Roger Ailes,
Oil and churches,
And wealthy John Birches,
Gun nuts and hawks,
Wars in Iraqs,
Weapons and lobbies,
Ahmad Chalabis,
Book of Genesis creation,
Social Security privatization,
SUVs,
Wine and cheese.

What are little Democrats made of?
Gay weddings,
Forgotten beheadings,
Trial lawyers,
And Bill Moyers,
Union bosses,
Election losses,
Experimental solar cars,
Self-centered movie stars,
Liberal elites,
Government teats,
Lack of spine,
Cheese and wine.

Jack's House

These are the men
That fleeced the tribes
That paid the money
That made the bribes
That purchased the Congress that Jack built.

This is the Duke
That sailed the yacht
That raised the eyebrows
And got him caught,
Who helped Mitch Wade,
Who bought Duke's land
And kicked in 700 grand;
Which raised Duke's taxes,
And gave Duke pain;
So Wade paid the tab
On Duke's capital gain.
Bigger than Abscam:
Randy "Duke" Cunningham!
Top gun in the Congress that Jack built.

This is Bob Ney,
Who knew the fine print
That could pass a casino
And rev up its mint,
Who spawned the e-mail

Where Jack foretold:
"Just met with Ney.
"We're [expletive] gold!"
And Ney in 2000,
A moment quite checkered
Ripped magnate Gus Boulis
In the *Congress'nal Record*.
His tirade was meant
To frighten the fellow,
Who cops say was shot
By Big Tony Moscatiello,
Who got a small fortune
From Jack's pal in D.C.,
A guy Ney said was known
For his "honesty."
Their pal was indicted
And then copped a plea
Guilty of fraud
And conspiracy.
For creating the vibes
That condoned the bribes
That corrupted the Congress that Jack built.

This is DeLay,
Who built the machine
That redrew the districts
And raised the green,
That decided the races
That claimed the new seats,

That made the new friends
That owned luxury suites,
That held big galas
That brought the donations
That helped him to greet
The great Coushatta Nation!
With 800 members
And fund-stream support
From the famous Coushatta Casino Resort!
Which paid several million
For Jack to abort
A rival tribe's parlor
In nearby Shreveport,
Which prompted the letter
That outlined their claims
That went to Gale Norton,
Cosigned by these names:
Tom DeLay, Eric Cantor,
Roy Blunt, the chief Whip,
Speaker Dennis Hastert.
That's the House leadership!
That played the game
And wears the shame
That hangs over the Congress that Jack built.

This is the Jack,
Jack Abramoff,
Who bought the souls,
Then sold them off,

Who shook the hands,
And financed the houses,
And feted the staffs,
And hired the spouses,
And fleeced the tribes,
And spread the bribes
That ransomed the Congress that Jack built.

Cyndi McKinney

Cyndi McKinney of the Congress band,
Marched into work without getting scanned.
"Stop!" yelled the cop, but away she ran;
Said Cyndi McKinney, "Catch me if you can!"

Cyndi McKinney just kept up her pace.
The cop shouted, "Stop!" and then gave chase.
He grabbed Cyndi's arm, then what did he say?
The cop cried, "Oww!" as Cyndi flailed away.

Cyndi McKinney threw fists high and low,
Then smacked him with her phone, like Russell Crowe.
Cyndi yelled, "I'm in Congress!" between each whack.
"And you're hassling me just because I'm black!"

Cyndi McKinney got nabbed that day,
And she even got denounced by Tom DeLay,
They still whine about her hair on FOX TV.
But when Cyndi goes to work, she flashes ID.

Cool James Inhofe

There is no global warming.
James Inhofe tells us so.
He's in from Oklahoma,
And knows how these things go.

There are no melting glaciers,
It's just the rising sea.
James Inhofe did the research,
With his bachelor's degree.

There are no monster hurricanes.
It's just some moving skies.
James Inhofe crunched the numbers.
The others just tell lies.

No greenhouse gas emissions.
It's just a faulty rule.
His donors from Big Oil
Assure him we'll stay cool.

No need for conservation.
James Inhofe leads the way.
Everything will be all right.
Keep burning, it's okay.

Big Jon Tester

Big Jon Tester of Montana,
Worst-est sight for rightward-wingers,
Big as a bear, Grace Jones hair,
Three hundred pounds and seven fingers.

Big Jon Tester of Montana,
Worst-est sight for mudward-slingers,
Took his turns, whupped Conrad Burns,
Three hundred pounds and seven fingers.

Big Jon Tester of Montana,
Worst-est sight for right humdingers,
Sunday suit, the beaut of Butte!
Three hundred pounds and seven fingers.

Little Lincoln Chaffee

Little Lincoln Chaffee,
Though not a Mellon Scaife,
Donned his Republican clothes,
The neocons booed him,
The Dems pooh-poohed him
Some days, that's just how it goes.

Little Lincoln Chaffee,
Couldn't spread enough gravy,
And stubbed his Republican toes,
His term elapsed,
And the big tent collapsed,
"The Party of Lincoln" . . . deposed.

A Shoemaker Makes Shoes

A shoemaker makes shoes without leather,
With four elements all together.
Sweat. Labor. Exploitation. Idea.
And all his shoes come from Korea.

A filmmaker makes films with much leather,
With four elements all together.
Fist fight. Shoot out. Car chase. Sex scene.
And all his films are PG-13.

A lawmaker writes laws of bellwether,
From four elements all together.
Donors. Donors. Donors. Donors.
And all his laws come from his owners.

Congress v. People

Congress health plan:
"Take your pick."
People's health plan:
"Don't get sick."

Congress wage plan:
"A little more, please."
People's wage plan:
"It grows on trees?"

Congress privacy:
"Our rights won't slide!"
People's privacy:
"Got something to hide?"

Congress probe:
"We found no paper trail."
People's probe:
"You're going to jail!"

Congress priorities:
"Get to that parade!"
People's priorities:
"Get the bills paid."

Congress pension:
"Golden years of wonder!"
People's pension:
"Six feet under."

Congress Iraq view:
"Our sons do care."
People's Iraq view:
"Our sons are there!"

Congress, Congress

Congress, Congress, "Stay the Course!"
Keep a large and steady force.
Never shall we set a date.
But let's get out by 2008.

Congress, Congress, "Cut and Run!"
By September, get it done.
After that, it's much too late.
But let's not wait 'til 2008.

Congress, Congress, mull this one:
Tell the Army "Eat and Run!"
Just go dining, plate to plate,
And then return way overweight.

Congress, Congress, tell the force:
We've decided, "Play the Course!"
Massive fairways we'll create,
And strive to keep our backswings straight.

Congress, Congress, one more tap:
How about we "Cut the Crap!"
Tell the truth before too late,
Or pay the price in 2008.

There Was a Crooked Man

There was a crooked man
Who walked a crooked mile,
He ran a crooked business,
Behind his crooked smile.

He joined a crooked party,
And made a crooked case,
He led a crooked ballot,
And won a crooked race.

He wrote a crooked measure,
That made a crooked law,
He banked a crooked million,
And made a crooked haul.

He helped a crooked donor,
Who hired his crooked spouse,
Now they all work together
In the nation's crooked House.

3.

"Clarence Thomas went to town
Dressed in his judicial gown"

The Court

Tony Scalia, Tony Scalia

Tony Scalia, Tony Scalia.
Is divine jurisprudence a worthy idea?
Does conventional law cover Jose Padilla?
Can inmates be force-fed a chicken tortilla?
And Anna Nicole . . .
　　What'd ya think? Mamma Mia!

David H. Souter, David H. Souter.
Can the government covertly seize my computer?
Can RICO Act statutes shut down a polluter?
Did President Bush take the right course with Scooter?
And Anna Nicole . . .
　　Well, wouldja ka-boot her?

Anthony Kennedy, Anthony Kennedy.
Should we get bar codes that prove our identity?
Does free speech negate certain rules of profanity?
Are Bibles in schools an unlawful amenity?
And Anna Nicole . . .
　　That was some femininity!

Stephen Breyer, Stephen Breyer.
Must nonprofits justify whom they will hire?
Should jurists . . . aww, heck—
　　Did she make you perspire?

Samuel Alito, Samuel Alito.
Did Anna Nicole fire up your libido?
John Paul Stevens, John Paul Stevens.
Did you happen to catch those incredible cleavin's?

Clarence Thomas, Clarence Thomas.
Do you think Anna wore lace pajamas?
John Roberts, Chief Justice John.
You think Anna had any underwear on?

Ruth Bader Ginsburg! Ruth Bader Gin—
Uhhhhhhhhh . . . well . . .
Under INS law, should ex-cons be let in?
Should quotas be based on the color of skin?
And Anna Nicole . . .
How the heck did she win?

4.

"Gores see polls and Doles see polls
And Lindsey Grahams see Bidens"

Candidates

Ten-Point Lead in May

A ten-point lead in May,
Your rival's quite okay.

A nine-point lead in June,
He's not one you'll impugn.

Eight points, July third.
Against him, not a word.

Five-point lead, late July,
Maybe time to wonder why.

Down to four, early August,
Time to note his daughter's drug bust.

Three points up, August eight.
Photoshop him, overweight.

Just two points on Labor Day.
Inquire why he hates to pray.

Two-point lead, September four.
Bash his service in the war.

One point up in October.
Whisper he's not staying sober.

Dead heat, October eight.
He's "the al-Qaeda candidate."

Down one, following morn,
Why's he soft on kiddie porn?

Down two, October thirty.
Now it's time to play dirty.

Dead heat, Election Day.
Shout it out: The guy is gay!

Mitt Romney

Mitt Romney,
Harmony nominee!
Family homily,
Kennedy enemy!

Mitt Romney,
Uncommon economy!
GOP dominee,
Matinee anatomy!

Mitt Romney,
Mormon anomaly!
Mention polygamy?
Primary calamity!

Clinton, Biden, and Dodd

Clinton, Biden, and Dodd one night
Sailed off in a wooden shoe—
Rode off on a river of crystal light,
Along with a hopeful few.
"Where are you going, and what do you wish?"
The old moon asked them all.
"We've come to find what new gibberish
"Will bring the greatest haul.
"And to answer our nation's call."
Said Clinton, Biden, et al.

The old moon laughed and sang a song,
As they rocked in the wooden shoe,
Reporters eyed them all night long
With their burgeoning cast and crew.
There came Kerry, Obama, and Richardson,
John Edwards and Al Gore.
"Just cast your nets wherever you wish,
"Your great campaigns will soar!"
So said the stars, in their nightly call,
To Clinton, Biden, et al.

All year long their campaigns pitched
To the stars of the media foam;
Then out to the prairie, where caucus crowds
Could ponder their rousing tomes;

'Twas all so hopeful a crowd it seemed
Like a beauty contestant corps,
And some even called it a fantasy
In the time of a hopeless war.
But each gave chase to the public's nod,
Clinton, Biden, and Dodd.

Clinton and Biden were tired loaves,
And the others were hardened bread,
And the wooden shoe that held their dreams
Was Dick Cheney's funeral bed.
So close your eyes while the nation sings
Of the wonderful ways of fate,
And dream of one person to save us all
In the year 2008,
When we see who answers the nation's call,
Of Clinton, Biden, et al.

Hey! Let's Vote Obama!

We don't know much about him.
We don't know what he's done.
We don't know what he stands for,
Or why he wants to run.
We don't know if he's able,
Or even if he's sane,
But, hey! let's vote Obama,
He looks good off the plane.

It could be he's dishonest,
Or maybe, really dense.
He might name Katie Couric
Secretary of Defense.
Or maybe he'll go crazy,
With several wars unfurled.
But, hey! let's vote Obama,
It's only just the world.

He might fall down like Jerry Ford,
Or bore us, like Al Gore,
Or in Japan, like old George Bush,
Puke sushi on the floor.
He might trade arms for hostages,
Then later not recall.
Or rant like Richard Nixon
To the paintings on the wall.

He might be weak like Carter,
Or be mean like LBJ,
He might have secrets in his past.
Who knows: He might be gay.
He'd undermine our allies,
A threat to global peace,
He might boost same-sex marriage,
Or, worse, a tax increase.

Or shred the Constitution,
Or leave our troops unpaid,
Sell nukes to North Korea,
Or even shag an aide!
Or bust our nation's budget,
Leave everything amiss,
But, hey! let's vote Obama,
He can't be worse than this.

Handsome Johnny

Handsome Johnny Edwards,
Such a winning style,
Not much on specifics,
But sure can spin a smile.

Handsome Johnny Edwards,
Leader of the team,
Not sure what he's saying,
But sure can talk a dream.

Handsome Johnny Edwards,
Answering the call,
A little vague on issues.
But truly loves us all.

Handsome Johnny Edwards,
Johnny on the spot,
Not sure what we're getting,
But Hillary, he's not.

Old John McCain

Old John McCain
Had a very fine brain
What a very fine brain had he,
He went to 'Nam,
Then he came back home,
And he ran with the GOP.
He reached for the sky,
And then faced the lie,
That a little bit nutty was he, was he,
Old John McCain is not insane,
Tweedle-dum-doo, tweedle-dee-dee.

Old John McCain,
Faced a harsh campaign,
From Bush in a primary spree,
The folks George hired,
Claimed that John sired,
And a little black baby had he,
He lost in the poll,
Then tore Bush a hole,
For a very big temper had he, had he,
Old John McCain felt great disdain,
Tweedle-dum-doo, tweedle-dee-dee.

New John McCain,
Is a-running again,

What a hungry old swain is he,
Now he backs the war,
And he says "Send more!"
And he and George Bush agree,
He chases the prize,
And in GOP eyes,
They all see what they want to see, to see,
Old John McCain has a new campaign,
Tweedle-dum-doo, tweedle-dee-dee.

Rememberin' Rudy

It's Rememberin' Rudy, America's Mayor.
Everywhere he goes, there's a memory there.
Remember his greatness after 9-1-1.
He's Rememberin' Rudy, Run, Rudy, Run!

It's Rememberin' Rudy, America's Glory.
Everywhere he goes, he remembers a story.
He gave us such hope that awful September.
Run, Rudy, run, And remember, remember!

It's Rememberin' Rudy, America's Smash.
Everywhere he goes, he remembers to raise cash.
He gave us such hope that horrible date.
Vote Rememberin' Rudy in 2008!

Little Ralph Reed

Little Ralph Reed has lost his creed
And doesn't know where to find it.
Leave him alone
For it's not known
If his flock was really behind it.

Little Ralph Reed was lost, indeed,
And dreamt his fortunes were righted.
But when he awakened
His prospects were shaken,
For some of his pals were indicted.

Little Ralph Reed had cast his seed
With the truth that came from the ballot.
Yet he prayed not for luck,
But the Almighty Buck
For, deep down, he preferred a thick wallet.

Little Ralph Reed had hoped to lead
As one whom the people put trust in,
But for all his grace
And his choirboy face,
He thanks God that the cops didn't bust him.

Schwarzenegger

Schwarzenegger sits in the White House tree.
Merry, merry friend of the Bush is he.
Laugh, Schwarzenegger,
Laugh with glee.
Have your gay friends met the GOP?

Schwarzenegger sits in Republican class,
Then pushes for cuts in greenhouse gas,
Laugh, Schwarzenegger,
Laugh the last,
Has Cheney noticed those laws you pass?

Schwarzenegger sips from the White House well,
Being pro-choice and pro–stem cell,
Laugh, Schwarzenegger,
Laugh and yell,
Do they ask about you, and do you tell?

The Cock Doth Crow

Hello, hello!
The cock doth crow!
George Allen says,
'Tis time to go!
"The day anew,
"Is calling you.
"I roar,
"Macaca-Doodle-Doo!"

Good day, good day!
The cock doth say!
George Allen says,
"Wake up! Oy vey!
"A morning dew,
"Is greeting you.
"I'm your
"Macaca-Doodle-Jew!"

Stay the Course

Stay the course!
Stay on your horse.
We won't cut and run.
Stay the course!
Show no remorse
Until the day we've won.

Stay the course!
A show of force.
Show everything's okay.
Stay the course!
Shout 'til you're hoarse.
And we will win the day.

Stay the course!
Keep at the source
It's hope we must instill.
Stay the course!
And *"No divorce!"*
Said Hillary to Bill.

Hillary Dillary Murdoch

Hillary Dillary Murdoch.
The spouse endorsed Iraq.
It turned unsettled
And back she pedaled.
Hillary Dillary Murdoch.

Hillary Dillary Rodham
The spouse backed ousting Saddam.
The insurgence churned
And 'round she turned.
Hillary Dillary Rodham.

Hillary Dillary Clinton.
The spouse spent time reprintin':
"This war is all wrong,
"As I knew all along!"
Hillary Dillary Clinton.

5.

"London Bridge might be falling down!
Falling down! Falling down!"

Media

The Pundit War

The world fell into darkness,
In the year 2008,
With war and death and famine
To decide the human fate.

The people of America,
Aft' all had gone askew,
Cried out in search of heroes,
And thus found the chosen few.

For they were blessed with champions,
Who vowed to win the war,
And so was formed the mighty
First Commando Pundit Corps.

They came from network TV,
Cable news, and government.
They'd reached a mighty stature
From their willingness to vent.

One by one, these warriors
Packed sprays and microphones,
These rock-ribbed tellers of hard truth
Then charged the battle zones!

Rush Limbaugh's men took Baghdad
In a hard-fought, two-day grab.
In triumph, he could mock the play
Of Donovan McNabb.

Keith Olbermann gave speeches
To the Army's upper brass.
They didn't use his plans
But powered convoys with his gas.

O'Reilly in the outskirts
Vowed his men would never waffle,
Then goofed and called the city
Not "Fallujah" but "Falafel."

Al Franken and Bob Novak
Told one-liners 'bout the Jews.
Arianna coaxed the local stars
To blog about their views.

Ann Coulter wore her miniskirt
In mosques and private homes.
Sean Hannity rode the streets
On top of Alan Colmes.

In a firestorm of sound bytes,
Bill Maher took Sadr City,
And all agreed that Brooks and Shields
Had never been more witty.

Brit Hume pitched bombs of candor,
Giant words did George Will string,
And Cokie Roberts sounded off
On *War with Larry King*.

In one mission, surrounded
And outnumbered ten to one,
Tim Russert asked tough questions.
The insurgents cut and run.

Once, holding out in Baghdad,
When they couldn't last too long,
The opposition wilted
When McLaughlin shouted, "Wrong!"

The terror forces rallied,
As the U.S. generals feared.
Our chances looked quite hopeless,
'Til a famous 'stash appeared!

That moment changed momentum,
And the pundits seized the day,
The Army stepped aside
And let Geraldo lead the way!

Then the hardened heroes,
Knew exactly what to say.
They all announced the war was won,
Then headed to L.A.

The Pundit Corps returned to crowds
With cheering and great glories,
Along with medals came the deals
For film rights to their stories.

And though the fighting overseas
Continued evermore,
The pundits were victorious in
The First World Ratings War.

The Miller's Tale

The Queen of Hacks,
Proclaimed some facts
Upon a summer's day.
The Times of York,
Ran her report,
On Saddam's war cache.

The King of State
Became irate,
And sent troops to Iraq.
The Blogs of Net,
Saw through the threat,
And said she wrote a crock.

The Queen of Hacks,
Faced harsh attacks,
But vowed she would prevail.
The Court of Law,
Said "Sources? Pshaw!"
And threatened her with jail.

The Queen of Hacks
Refused to wax
And vowed to fight for rights.
The Judge of Court

Scorned her retort,
And jailed her eighty nights.

The Kings of Court
Cut her time short
And gave her a vacation,
The York of Times,
Denied all crimes,
But took her resignation.

Memo to Employees

Memo to employees:
Scrutinize the wires.
Look for some insurgents
Dancing round their fires.
Say they're celebrating,
The Democrats' big day.
Remember: Fair and balanced
Is the FOX News way.

Memo to employees:
Watch for any news
Of Pelosi in Armani
And three-hundred-dollar shoes.
Mention how she's wealthy
In everything you say,
Remember: Fair and balanced
Is the FOX News way.

Memo to employees:
Watch for any speech
That Howard Dean should utter,
Then play his famous screech.
Mention Kerry's soldier joke
Twenty times today.
Remember: Fair and balanced
Is the FOX News way.

Memo to employees:
Take this as a threat.
Someone's leaking memos
On the Internet.
I will catch this culprit,
He or she will pay,
Telling how things are
Is not the FOX News way.

Billy Clinton Went to FOX

Billy Clinton went to FOX,
Looking for some ears to box.
Young Chris Wallace said, "Hello."
And Billy cried, "*Okay! Let's go!*"

Billy Clinton, on his way to lunch,
Beckoned Chris to throw a punch.
"Why'd you blow it?" Chris inquired,
And folks still mull what next transpired.

Billy Clinton gave a sigh,
And looked the newsman in his eye.
"You dare say my record's bad?
"Listen, son, you're not your dad."

Billy Clinton wagged his fingers,
"How come you don't grill right-wingers?"
"You don't question Bush's fouls!
"You don't bug the Colin Powells!

"You don't question Rumsfeld's part!
"Or ever pressure Cheney's heart!
"You don't tussle Condoleezza!
"You just bow and beg to please 'er!

"You don't ask the price we've paid!
"You're still mad 'cause I got laid!
"You just pass on Karl Rove's tales!
"You're a sponge for Roger Ailes!"

Billy Clinton in his chair,
Gave his host a baleful stare.
"But, sir," Chris said, his eyebrows working.
"Shut your trap!" Bill said. "Stop smirking!"

Billy Clinton showed disdain,
Then left to pimp his wife's campaign,
Chris just sat there, smiling sly,
As his ratings touched the sky.

Rock-a-Bye, Katie

Rock-a-bye, Katie,
In the big chair,
Though the news breaks,
The headline's your hair.

If the bombs fall
And world wars begin,
They'll still talk of Katie,
And how she's so thin.

Rock-a-bye Katie,
In the storm breeze,
Through the Cat-5
They peek at your knees.

When the world ends,
The stories will file,
And there will be Katie,
Known for her smile.

On Top of Old Morley

On top of old Morley
All covered with gray,
It lasts *60 Minutes*,
It seems a whole day.

There's old Andy Rooney,
You thought he retired,
He's still on the air, though,
He cannot be fired.

Reporters so old, dear.
Reporters so old.
They'll keel at their desks, dear,
Reporters so old.

And then there's Mike Wallace,
Still with that fake tan,
He's soon pushing ninety,
His son's an old man.

They shelled out for Katie,
Young viewers she'd save,
But the old-time reporters,
Keep filin' from the grave.

And a weak-hearted news show
Is worse than a thief.
Like chewing Viagra
Without any teeth.

Reporters so old, dear.
Reporters so old.
Good night and good luck, dear.
Reporters so old.

Thin Annie Coulter

Annie Coulter gained no weight,
Despite the many things she ate.

She stayed as skinny as a rail,
Although she dined on Cheney's quail.

She thinned herself to twelve-inch thighs,
Devouring Joe McCarthy's lies.

She always stayed so very trim,
Yet ate Max Cleland's missing limb.

She looked just like a stalk of hay,
But ate the bombs of Tim McVeigh.

She kept her weight so very low,
Yet swallowed lines from Tony Snow.

Though slender as a nylon thread,
She feasted on Iraqi dead.

She just resembled skin and bones,
Yet ate the claims of Paula Jones.

Her arms were wires; her legs were spokes.
Yet she gorged on "faggot" jokes.

She grew so thin we almost lost her,
Yet ate the death of Vincent Foster.

She swallowed Democratic lives.
She swallowed 9/11 wives.

You wonder how Ann kept her looks?
She crapped her meals into her books.

Little Tim Russert

Little Tim Russert sat in his dress shirt,
Letting Dick Cheney talk,
The GOP vice
Sought to make nice,
And claimed things were swell in Iraq.

Little Tim Russert bowed to the expert,
Barely making a squeak,
His famous guest
Denied any mess,
Until finally Tim rose to speak.

Little Tim Russert put forth some bluster,
And Cheney's lips were squeezed.
Three questions tough,
The guest cried, "Enough."
And both went home quite pleased.

Oprah Winfrey Sat on a Chair

Oprah Winfrey sat on the chair.
Oprah Winfrey gave a great glare.
All of the author's attempts to pretend,
Couldn't put James Frey together again.

Oprah Winfrey sat on the wall,
Oprah Winfrey gave a great haul,
All in the crowd that day to attend,
Got a new car, for being her friend.

Oprah Winfrey stood on the scale.
Oprah Winfrey gave a great wail.
All the show's doctors and all the show's men,
Couldn't put Oprah in size six again.

Lou Dobbs

I've heard a killer asteroid
Is waiting out in space.
I've heard that global warming
Will destroy the human race.
I've heard the bird flu virus
Could turn cities into mobs.
But I will not believe it
'Til I hear it from Lou Dobbs.

I've heard the Midwest climate
Soon could be too hot for grain.
I've heard use of cell phones
Can cause cancer of the brain.
I've heard the next depression
Will cost everyone their jobs,
But I will not believe it
'Til I hear it from Lou Dobbs.

I've heard Lou Dobbs is angry
That illegals get on through,
I've heard Lou Dobbs has written up
A plan to stop the flu,
I've heard Lou Dobbs is fighting
For us losers and us slobs,
And this I do believe,
Because I heard it from Lou Dobbs.

I Have a Little Weblog

I have a little Weblog,
They want you to ignore.
Each day I expose their lies
Some sixteen times or more.

I write about conspiracies,
Pure fact, without dramatics,
To sabotage the evil schemes
Of rich right-wing fanatics.

It started in the '90s,
Their plan to seize control.
They'd lost the big election
With their robot, Robert Dole.

Rumsfeld, once a drug exec,
With Karl Rove as his flunky,
Got his hands on some Viagra,
Which made old white guys spunky.

They fed it to Dick Cheney,
And then to Andy Card,
Who got inside the White House,
And slipped some to a guard.

From there it got to Clinton,
Who never had a chance.
He took ten thousand milligrams
And burst out of his pants.

They fed it to the Bushes,
One evening in Rhode Island.
George and Jeb found Jesus.
Neil ran amok in Thailand.

They gave some pills to Saddam,
To pump up strained relations,
They dished them out to cheery hosts
On a.m. talk-show stations.

They hooked the Pope and Bono,
And Britain's Tony Blair.
They fed the howl of Howard Dean
And then John Kerry's hair.

They fed Greta van Susteren,
Who got a brand new face.
They gave some to a lawyer,
Who turned into Nancy Grace.

Alan Greenspan tried some;
Andrea Mitchell offered thanks.
They sent some to the Red Sox
Who then spanked the New York Yanks.

They juiced up poor Dan Rather,
Whose staff grew so engorged,
He broadcast some documents
That someone may have forged.

They sent pills out to voters
In Florida's elections.
They raised a public groundswell
Of Republican erections.

They blinded half the country,
Old rich men chasing females.
Then someone blew the secret:
I got offers in my e-mails.

Now Rumsfeld's drug is everywhere,
We're lost inside its fog.
But I take two each hour,
It gives me strength to blog.

6.

"Eighty deaths hath September
Sixty more in November"

Iraq

Saddam Saddam

Saddam, Saddam, the viper son,
Stole Baghdad, and away he run,
Launched a war,
Against Iran,
So Rumsfeld came,
And shook his hand.

Saddam, Saddam, the scoundrel one,
Left Baghdad, and away he run.
Dug a hole,
Way down deep,
Got caught up in
A morning sweep.

Saddam, Saddam, the hated one,
In Baghdad, with pajamas on,
Went on trial,
Yelled all day,
Thought he'd never
Go away.

Saddam, Saddam, the vanquished one,
Near Baghdad, with a noose undone,
Hung at dawn,
Claimed no regret,
His final place,
The Internet.

How Many Miles to Babylon?

How many miles to Babylon?
Three score and ten.
Can we get there by April first?
Aye! And back again!
There's no reason why we'd stay.
We'll be home by first of May.

How many miles to Babylon?
Two score and ten.
Can we get there by late June?
Aye! We're sure we can.
Nothing more shall go awry,
We'll be home by mid-July.

How many miles to Babylon?
One score and ten.
Can we get there by October?
Uh, well . . . it depends.
Soon, our foes shall surely splinter,
We'll be home by early winter.

How many miles to Babylon?
Please don't ask again.
When's the soonest we get home?
Well . . . 2010.
All our hopes have been withdrawn,
There may not be a Babylon.

Jill and Jack

Jill and Jack went to Iraq
To topple a dictator.
Jill got hit in east Tikrit.
And Jack went back to save her.

Jill and Jack went back to Iraq,
To make conditions better.
Jill hit the wall in west Karbala.
And Jack went back to get her.

Jill and Jack found they had to go back
In the Army's "Stop-Loss" writing.
They found Jill's body in Ramadi,
And Jack's still out there, fighting.

When You're In, You're In

When you're in, you're in,
And when you're out, you're out,
'Cause once you send your Army in,
It's hard to pull it out.

When you're up, you're up,
And when you're down, you're down,
And when the deaths are going up,
Your polls are going down.

'Cause when you lose, you lose,
And when you win, you win,
And when you can't tell win from lose,
Best stop the war you're in.

Little Boy Blair

Little boy Blair,
Come wear your scorn.
Iraq's in the gutter,
Iran's on the horn.
Where's the Churchill
Of 2003?
He's dodging attacks
On the BBC.

Little boy Blair,
Come stop the war.
You might have done better
With President Gore.
Where's the young leader
Whose belly held fire?
They now spell your name
"Tony B-Liar."

Little boy Blair,
Come hear the hordes.
You're taking abuse
In the House of Lords.
Where's the young man
Who fought against terror?
He's stuck in Iraq,
Still tied to his error.

Henry and the War

Henry Kissinger met the war,
And said, "How do you do?"
The two sat down, and Henry said,
"I do remember you!"

They talked a bit, then Henry said,
"It's been a long, long while."
He gave the war a playful squeeze,
The war returned his smile.

Henry Kissinger beamed with joy,
And the two strolled hand-in-hand.
He knew he'd found his long-lost mate,
And the war had found its man.

Pat-a-Cake

Pat-a-cake, pat-a-cake, Baker man,
Make our escape as fast as you can.
Think it, and write it, and show it to the D's
Then put it to the Congress for Cheney and me!

Pat-a-cake, pat-a-cake, Baker group.
Fix our mistakes, we're deep in the soup.
Roll it, heal it, mark it "B" for bad,
Just get me out of this, like you did with Dad.

Pat-a-cake, pat-a-cake, Baker crew.
What did you think I wanted from you?
Drop it, forget it; just please take a walk.
You'll make folks think that it's bad in Iraq.

Leaving

"If we leave, they'll follow us."
George Bush's words ring true.
That doesn't leave us many outs,
So here's what we should do:

Secretly, we pack our bags,
Then one day, before dawn,
We cut loose for the airports,
A hundred-thousand strong.

First, we fly to Cairo,
We stay a day or two,
Then, leaving all the TVs on,
We sneak out to Peru.

We occupy for several days,
Pretending to take classes,
Then in one great movement,
We deploy fake mustaches.

We fly to Britain, boat to Spain,
Don dresses in the lavs,
At four a.m., we hit the roads,
We all take separate cabs.

We stop in Venezuela,
Knock Chavez off his can,
We check if someone's following,
Then back to Spain again.

We hover for three hours,
Then double back once more,
Euro Disney, then straight home,
That's how we end the war.

7.

"Diddle, diddle dumpling, my son John
Talks online with his congressman"

Issues

Little Bo Peep

Little Bo Peep has cloned her sheep
And doesn't know if to mind it.
If here or there
She doesn't care,
She's got bigger fears behind it.

Little Bo Peep's into cloning deep
Though few folks know about it.
She'll snatch a cell
And never tell,
Then clone the thing and sprout it.

Little Bo Peep has cloned D.C.,
Planned by her clone, Karl Rove.
She did John McCain
From a piece of a brain
That was found in Pat Robertson's stove.

Little Bo Peep then cloned the Veep
While hunting quail down South.
She smiled a lot,
Ducked when he shot,
And scored spit from Cheney's mouth.

Little Bo Peep cloned every street
In Washington's Beltway zone.

She cloned Denny Hastert
From a hair on the plaster
Just over Mark Foley's phone.

Little Bo Peep went on a spree,
Cloning the best and worst.
She cloned Claire McCaskill
From a strange-looking toenail
In Hillary Clinton's purse.

Little Bo Peep cloned folks for free.
She did the work by feel.
She cloned Jim Webb
From a small chunk of Jeb
That she merged with some Danielle Steel.

Little Bo Peep sometimes made a creep,
And barely averted disaster.
She cloned a Bill Frist
From a hair on the wrist
Of Terry Schiavo's pastor.

Little Bo Peep then took a great leap
Even though she barely had to.
She cloned Tom DeLay
With some merged DNA
From Roy Blunt and the late Spiro Agnew.

Little Bo Peep can't get to sleep.
Her creations have rocked her beliefs.
She cloned Joe Biden
From a hair that was hidin'
In Barack Obama's briefs.

Little Bo Peep got in too deep
When her copies got overgrown.
Her fake generation
Is running the nation,
And that's why we banned the clone.

It's Raining, It's Pouring

It's raining, it's storming,
The planet is warming.
The FEMA head
Has gone to bed
And tropical storms are forming.

It's raining, it's hailing,
We ought to be bailing.
Michael Brown
Is joking around
And the levee system is failing.

It's raining, it's pelting,
The ice caps are melting.
The President's style
Is in denial
And waterways are swelling.

It's raining, it's pouring!
The planet's Al Goreing.
See who'll survive
Our next Cat-5
And hope that nobody's snoring.

Do Your Teeth Hang Low?

Do your teeth hang low?
Do you wobble to and fro?
Is your bladder in a knot?
Are you leaky down below?
Can you barely lift your shoulder?
Are you older than a boulder?
Do your teeth hang low?

Do your bills run high?
Monthly payments to the sky?
Have you hit the donut hole?
Are you making plans to die?
Do the Medicare descriptions
Leave you passing up prescriptions?
Do your bills run high?

Are you feeling tricked?
Are your pockets nice and picked?
Did you buy their lies,
Though you knew they'd contradict?
Are prescription payments higher
As you're hoping to retire?
Are you feeling tricked?

Higglety, Pigglety, My Brown Maid

Higglety, pigglety, my brown maid,
Doesn't know she's underpaid.
Never files a jobless claim.
Someday I will learn her name.
Many nights, she even cooks,
Best part is, she's off the books.
For her love I've often prayed.
Higglety, pigglety, my brown maid.

Higglety, pigglety, my hired hand.
Hails from some non-English land.
Makes the bus to work on time.
Knows that unions are a crime.
Saves each dollar that he earns,
Hauls away our bottle returns.
Broken arm? He knows he's canned.
Higglety, pigglety, my hired hand.

Higglety, pigglety, these damn aliens,
None of them, Episcopalians.
They don't love our presidents.
We should build a taller fence.
Stealing all our children's jobs,
Don't you ever watch Lou Dobbs?
Higglety, pigglety, make a stand.
But save my maid and hired hand.

Albert, Put the Kettle On

Albert, put the kettle on,
Albert, put the kettle on,
Albert, put the kettle on,
Let's have tea!

George, take it off again,
George, take it off again,
George, take it off again,
Don't you see?

Heat the ocean one degree,
Add ten inches to the sea.
End of time for you and me.
Let's skip tea.

Boil the planet, burn the roast,
Melt the ice caps, flood the coast,
Blow the place, and we are toast,
Let's skip tea.

If Wishes Were Oil

If wishes were oil,
We all could drive Audis,
If turnips fueled cars,
We could flip off the Saudis.

If wishes were cash,
We all could have lackeys,
If turnips fueled cars,
We could leave the Iraqis.

If wishes were ice cream,
We'd all have four scoops,
If turnips fueled cars,
We could bring back the troops.

If wishes were wealth,
We would never do chores,
If turnips fueled cars,
We would not need these wars.

If wishes were deeds,
We would always do good.
If turnips fueled cars . . .
Wait a minute. They could!

Hey, Google-Google

Hey, Google-Google,
No need to be frugal,
The Dow jumped over the moon.
Wall Street waited,
To hear the pop,
And the bubble became a balloon.

Hey, Google-Google,
Search "kit and caboodle,"
The earth, the sun, and the moon.
Ten billion here,
Ten billion there,
And the dish ran away with the spoon.

To Market, To Market

To market, to market, an iPod to buy,
Home again, home again, jiggety-jy!
To market, to buy it an iPod iBase,
And then a protective black leather iCase.

To market, so my iPhones don't unravel,
An iTrip transmitter to go when I travel.
To market, to keep up a proper iZone,
I'll add an iKitchen and wooden iThrone.

To market, to boost its efficiency rate,
A new iPod Nano to be its iMate.
They'll have an iPuppy, a cuddly iHound,
With a little iHouse in a quiet iTown.

To market, so they can all live in iPeace,
I'll train some iDoctors and then iPolice.
With iTown officials for each situation,
I'll build for my iPod a perfect iNation.

To market, and if they face foreign attack,
I'll raise an iArmy, so they can fight back.
I'll secretly, covertly, launch the construction
Of scary iWeapons of iMass Destruction.

To market, to market, for all that it's worth,
My perfect iEmpire will rule its iEarth,
And I will be owner of all it transverses,
The iMaster King of the iUniverses.

To market, to market, but something is wrong.
My iPod is frozen, my iTunes are gone.
The iScreen won't brighten, the wheel won't unlock.
I've wasted my time. It's a total iRaq.

Blah, Blah, Blackberry

Blah, blah, Blackberry,
Have you any mail?
Yes, sir. Yes, sir.
Eight-point scale.

Spam from My Yahoo,
Spam from MySpace,
Spam from a site
Called "Ask Leatherface."

Spam from Time Warner.
Spam from My Page.
Spam from a site
Called "Kids Underage."

Spam for Cialis.
Spam for some stocks.
Spam for a book
By Ana Marie Cox.

Spam from My Google.
Spam in disguise.
Spam to expand
My manhood size.

Spam from PayPal.
Spam from a scam.
Spam from a site
That eliminates spam.

Blah, blah, Blackberry,
Any did you read?
No, sir. No, sir.
Delete, delete.

Tony Pellicano

Tony Pellicano, sittin' in a tree.
Taping Liz Hurley from her SUV.
Tony takes the money,
And he taps her phone.
Hey, look.
Now he's spying on Sly Stallone!

Tony Pellicano, sittin' in the wild,
Taping Michael Jackson's favorite boy child,
Tony takes the money,
And he looks real mean.
Hey, look.
Now he's spying on Keith Carradine!

Tony Pellicano, workin' on a schmooze,
Taping Nicole Kidman as she split from Tom Cruise.
Tony takes the money,
And sets his device.
Hey, look.
Now he's spying on Heidi Fleiss!

Tony Pellicano, sittin' in hell,
Taping news clippings to the walls of his cell.
Tony took the money,
And he spread the smut.
Hey, look.
Now he's spying on his cellmate's butt!

Kim Jung Il Built a Fine New Hall

Kim Jung Il built a fine new hall,
Pastry and piecrust formed the wall;
A floor of chocolate, black and white,
Roofed by a cloud that kept out light.

Kim Jung Il never left his place,
So no one else ever saw his face.
He lived alone, without a qualm,
And then one day he built a bomb.

Kim Jung Il said with great delight,
"Now the whole world knows my might."
He looked in the mirror, there to see,
The face of the king he'd hoped to be.

Kim Jung Il is no longer shy,
And stands in his hall of pastry and pie,
There with his bomb, he feels so tall,
Beneath the cloud that now covers us all.

The Muslim Man

Do you know the Muslim man?
The Muslim man, the Muslim man?
Do you know the Muslim man
Who lives on Drury Lane?

What do you know about the Muslim man?
The Muslim man, the Muslim man?
Have you had personal dealings with the Muslim man
Who lives on Drury Lane?

Do you know any friends of the Muslim man?
The Russian man? The Mexican?
Do they have immigration papers, these Latino men?
How often are they seen on Drury Lane?

We have reason to believe you are an associate of the
        Muslim man,
The Muslim man, the Muslim man.
We're taking you to see the Question Man.
You're leaving Drury Lane.

Barber, Barber, Shave a Pig

Barber, barber, shave a pig.
Make him watch; he'll flip his wig.
Forty hours, that's enough.
How long standing in the buff?

Jailer, jailer, shave his beard.
Later, claim he volunteered.
Remember, they serve endless time,
Never charged for any crime.

Warden, warden, save the heat.
Keep them cold and in bare feet.
And every hour, on the quarter,
Do those things we do with water.

Lawyer, lawyer, save our skins.
Indemnify us from our sins.
Once they're placed in our dominion,
Pain is good, in your opinion?

People, people, save our souls.
When does this promote our goals?
Is it right to turn the screw?
Or are we judged by what we do?

Life-Ender Blue

Threat Level *blue,* dilly, dilly.
No terror strife.
We won't see blue, willy-nilly,
Not in this life.

Threat Level *yellow,* dilly, dilly.
Terror at bay.
Try to stay mellow, willy-nilly.
Scared every day.

Threat Level *orange,* dilly, dilly.
Terror severe.
Lie down and cringe, willy-nilly.
Savor the fear.

Threat Level *red,* dilly, dilly.
Hell has been loosed.
We're going to die, willy-nilly.
Or Bush needs a boost.

Happy Acts

The White House experts sought a pact
To keep detainee rules intact.
So they wrote with stately tact
The "Happy Muslim Prisoner Act."

They also wanted to transform
How undercover cops perform.
So privacy is less the norm
With "Happy Tapping Phones Reform."

They sought to save their weary nation
Enduring Freedom's operation.
So they wrote a new creation,
The "Happy War Debt Legislation."

In fighting for that higher purpose,
They dismantled habeas corpus.
Thus wrote without internal rumpus
The "Happy Secret Trials Opus."

They sought to make the world less shrill,
While raising up their campaign till
So billionaires could give their fill,
The "Happy Lobby Gifting Bill."

They sought to do the best for all
And keep their faithful standing tall.
The rest they'd lock behind a wall
With the "Happy War Forever Law."

I See the Cams

I see the cams,
And the cams see me.
The cams see everyone
The cams should see.

I miss some cams,
But the cams see me.
The cams go everywhere
The cams should be.

I like the cams,
And the cams agree.
And the cams watch everything
To safeguard me.

I know each cam
Goes to some TV,
And I wonder how that cam
Is showing me.

I'll wink to cams.
They don't wink to me.
Sometimes I fear a cam sees
My privacy.

I'll miss a cam
Then I'll catch myself,
And wonder if the cam saw
Me scratch myself.

I know the cams
Can't be in my home,
Yet I even watch for them
While on the throne.

God bless the cams!
That's all I will say.
I just hope the cams show
That I'm Okay.

One for You, One for Me

Construction job.
A Catholic Church,
The site of God's Communion.
A buck for you.
A buck for me.
A buck for the labor union.

Brand new school.
A bus garage,
With many new additions.
A buck for you.
A buck for me.
A buck for the politicians.

New streets and curbs.
The power grid,
To shrink the Iraqi burden.
A buck for you.
A buck for me.
And ten for Halliburton.

If All the World Were Paper

If all the world were paper,
And all the sea were ink,
If all the news
Were one man's views,
What would we have to think?

If all the men were Limbaughs,
With wives as Helen Thomas,
With fights that dawned
And kids they spawned,
Would folks be wrong to bomb us?

If all the men were Cheneys,
And all their aides were Roves,
If every shore,
We fought a war,
Would we find weapons troves?

If all the men were Clintons,
And so were all their spouses,
With all their schemes
And all their dreams,
Would all deserve White Houses?

If all the world were holy,
And all religions one,
If everywhere
Found one same prayer,
Would God decide He's done?

8.

"Halle Berry, shave a pig
How many films in that X-Man wig?"

Celebrities

Star Lite, Star Brite

Star light, star bright,
First star I see tonight,
I wish I may,
I wish I might,
Get a star's support tonight.

Vanna White, Bob Knight,
Maybe Loudon Wainwright,
I wish one may,
I wish one might,
Visit my campaign tonight.

Sheryl Crow, J-Lo,
Steve-O, Fabio.
It's never you,
Just who you know,
That gives your race a healthy glow.

Liz Phair, Linda Blair,
That Doobie brother with the hair,
A famous name,
That's all they care.
So every day I e-mail Cher.

Joan Jett, David Arquette
Any former New York Met.

Richard Gere,
He'd be a "get,"
If we could keep him off Tibet.

Star blight, star poor,
I hoped at least for Pauly Shore.
No stars came.
I stay obscure.
Tonight, just me and Albert Gore.

Billy Bennett

Billy Bennett wrote the tenet,
Every parent must obey:
For your child to win a pennant,
He must first know how to pray.

Billy Bennett was resplendent,
Lifting families up to par.
His ideals became ascendant,
He became the Virtues Czar.

Billy Bennett, independent,
Kept a hidden secret muse,
He would clutch his lucky pendant,
Praying, *"Papa needs new shoes!"*

Billy Bennett, poker tenant,
In one Vegas weekend stand,
Threw the dice down, unrepentant,
And blew a cool 500 grand.

Billy Bennett, truth lieutenant,
Faced his critics hard and fair.
He said, there's no need to spin it,
If you're rich, God doesn't care.

Billy Bennett vowed to end it.
One great lesson had been learned:
A lucky fellow can transcend it,
If he's got the cash to burn.

Billy Bennett stayed resplendent,
As he tended to his flocks,
Though he'd never make the Senate,
He maintained his gig on FOX.

Mel Gibson Drank a Few

Mel Gibson drank a few
And swerved his car through Malibu.
An L.A. cop pulled into view,
And Mel asked, "Hey, are you a Jew?"

At the jailhouse Mel did more,
He urinated on the floor.
And to his hosts, he loudly swore,
That "F_____g Jews" cause every war.

Shouting taunts with merry wit,
Mel added to his words with spit
And gave one sergeant special fits,
By labeling her "Sugar Tits"!

Next day headlines bore the news:
"The Road Warrior" wrecked by booze!
And from his spokesman, sorrow oozed,
For Melvin Gibson loves the Jews.

But from the ramblings in his cell,
And shouts from his tequila hell,
The Semites of the world did tell,
The Passion—not of Christ, but Mel.

The Trinity

Lohan, Hilton, and Spears: Dear God!
It's Pestilence, Hunger, and Strife.
The cracks in our cultural brain façade,
And they'll probably be here for life.

Lohan, Hilton, and Spears: Dear Lord!
It's Sickness and Darkness and Death.
They're out on the town and looking bored,
And the tabloids record every breath.

Lohan, Hilton, and Spears: Oh, friends!
It's Cleavage and Cheesecake and Hair.
Two open their legs to the camera lens
Every time they sit down in a chair.

Lohan, Hilton, and Spears: Enough!
It's Make-up and Padding and Lips.
Oh, no: they just met with Hilary Duff.
The Four Tarts of the Apocalypse!

Teddy Foo-Foo

Pastor Teddy Foo-Foo,
I don't want to see you,
Preachin' that voodoo,
All the scary things you say.
I'll give you three chances,
But watch those glances,
'Cause if you keep them up,
I'll tell 'em
    You're gay!

Pastor Teddy Foo-Foo,
I don't want to see you,
Preachin' all that you do,
Those things you say of death.
I'll give you three chances,
But watch those advances,
'Cause if you keep them up,
I'll tell about
    The meth!

Pastor Teddy Foo-Foo,
I really hate to see you,
Preachin' with the Bush crew,
You're such a righteous star.
Here's your last chance.

Don't make an advance.
'Cause if you don't confess,
I'll tell 'em
Who you are!

A-Riddle: Who Am I?

In spring I do well,
And in June, I excel,
All summer, my output is keen.
When colder it grows,
My uncertainty shows,
And in autumn, I'm one for fourteen.

In April I soar,
Through July, my friends score,
All summer, I'm high as the sky.
Then comes the post,
When I'm needed the most,
And in autumn, not one RBI.

I rumble through June,
And they pay me the moon,
All summer, my teammates show faith.
Then the leaves start to fall,
And my stick becomes small,
And in autumn, they bat me at eighth.

Barry, Barry

Barry, Barry, quite contrary,
How does your body grow?
With "the cream" and "the clear" twelve times
    a year,
And testicles high in tow.

Barry, Barry, quite millionary,
How do you bring such awe?
With growth hormone and testosterone,
And breasts that need a bra.

Barry, Barry, quite extraordinary,
Why do you take such risks?
With urine purges and roidal urges
And records with asterisks.

9.

"Peter Pace picked a peck of pickled problems"

Coda

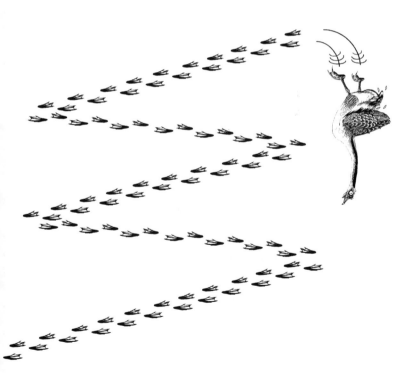

Can You Say This? 1.

Big-bucks bankers back Bush brother–backer brokers better!

But if big-bucks Bush brother–backers broker bitter bettors,
Would bitter big-bucks bankers break big-bucks Bush
brother–backer bettors' backs?

Can You Say This? 2.

What about W so troubles you?
Don't W's troubles trouble you, too?

If W throttles a bundle of vandals,
You belittle his mettle and grumble his scandals.

If W drubs a contemptible pooh-bah,
You grub-up a club and attempt a new hoo-ha.

If W fumbles a deficit decimal,
You rumble your warble to double the decibel.

If W rubbles a tower of Babel,
You cobble up trouble to sour the rabble.

If W crumbles one pebble of gravel,
You quibble and hobble the nub of his gavel.

If W cobbles a Nobel from Kabul,
You grumble and huddle a cartel and squabble.

If W paddles a do-little tattle,
You rattle his prattle as lickspittle drivel.

What about W so troubles you?
Don't W's troubles trouble you, too?

Can You Say This? 3.

John Kerry was a bear.
John Kerry had nice hair.
John Kerry was no Harry Carey . . . very

John Kerry backed Iraq.
John Kerry took it back.
John Kerry was a very airy, wary hara-kiri.

ACKNOWLEDGMENTS

For their encouragement, guidance, and occasional wise-ass remarks, I would be a total clod loser if I did not thank Bruce Nichols, David McCormick, Toby Harshaw, David Plotz, Michael Newman, Frank Cammuso, Tom Peyer, my fellow detainees at the Syracuse *Post-Standard,* and the soldiers of the U.S. Army's 10th Mountain Division, who took me to Iraq and then showed me the heart of America. Stay safe, all of you.

ABOUT THE AUTHOR

Hart Seely is an award-winning reporter for the Syracuse *Post-Standard.* His humor and satire have appeared in *The New Yorker, The New York Times, The Los Angeles Times, National Lampoon*, and on National Public Radio. He is the editor of *Pieces of Intelligence: The Existential Poetry of Donald H. Rumsfeld* and coeditor (with Tom Peyer) of *O Holy Cow! The Selected Verse of Phil Rizzuto*. Seely lives in beautiful Syracuse, New York, with his wife and three children.